C000039500

N

Karl Sydow in association with Natural Perspective,
Supporting Wall and Southwark Playhouse presents

Our Ajax

a new play by Timberlake Wertenbaker

World premiere at Southwark Playhouse, London,
on Friday 8th November 2013.

Production supported by the Unity Theatre Trust.

Our Ajax

Cast *in alphabetical order*

Frances Ashman	*Tecmessa*
Gemma Chan	*Athena*
Oliver Devoti	*Company Sergeant Major*
Joe Dixon	*Ajax*
James Kermack	*Soldier*
Jordan Mifsud	*Soldier*
William Postlethwaite	*Teucer*
Adam Riches	*Odysseus*
John Schwab	*Menelaos*
Fiona Skinner	*Soldier*
Douglas Wood	*Child*

Director	David Mercatali
Designer	James Turner
Lighting Designer	Christopher Nairne
Sound Designer	Max Pappenheim
Casting	Annie Rowe
Stage Manager	Ben Karakashian
Assistant Directors	Tom Latter
	Kate Morrison-Wynne
Education Assistant	Sophie George-Moore

Biographies

Frances Ashman | Tecmessa

Frances trained at the Guildhall School of Music and Drama and has since appeared in a variety of stage and television productions. Theatre work includes: *People* (National Theatre), *Bang Bang Bang* (Royal Court), *Pornography* (Birmingham Rep and Tricycle), *Cockroach* (National Theatre of Scotland), *Zuva Crumbling* (Lyric Hammersmith) and *Macbeth*, *Pericles* and *The Winter's Tale* (all RSC). On television Frances has been seen in: *Mayday*, *The Reckoning*, *Doctor Who*, *Law and Order UK*, *Missing*, *Trial and Retribution* and *Gunrush*.

Gemma Chan | Athena

Gemma trained at the Drama Centre London after graduating in law from Oxford University.

Theatre includes: *Yellow Face* (Park Theatre), *Turandot* (Hampstead Theatre), *The Sugar-Coated Bullets of the Bourgeoisie* (Finborough Theatre) and *Hey Brother* (Finborough Theatre).

Television includes: *Dates* (Channel 4), *Sherlock* (BBC), *Secret Diary of a Call Girl* (Showtime/ITV), *Fresh Meat* (Channel 4), *Doctor Who* (BBC), *True Love* (BBC), *Shetland* (BBC), *Bedlam* (Sky), *The IT Crowd* (Channel 4), *Death in Paradise* (BBC), *Mummy's Boys* (Comedy Central) and *The Game* (BBC).

Film includes: *Jack Ryan*: *Shadow Recruit* (dir. Kenneth Branagh), *The Double* (dir. Richard Ayoade), *Submarine* (dir. Richard Ayoade), *London Fields* (dir. Mathew Cullen), *Shanghai* (dir. Mikael Hafstrom) and *Exam* (dir. Stuart Hazeldine).

Oliver Devoti | Company Sergeant Major

This is Oliver's first time performing at Southwark Playhouse. A former infantry soldier, Oliver became an actor after leaving military service and training at Manchester School of Theatre (MMU), graduating in 2011. He has recently completed filming on George Clooney's *The Monument Men* (Smokehouse Productions/20th Century Fox) due for theatrical release in January 2014. Other credits include: *Desire Under the Elms* (Stoke New Vic), *Sherica* (MTA Winner 2011, Library Theatre/ Edinburgh Fringe/247 Festival), *One Hand Clapping* (House of Orphans/ IABF, Tomorrow/Appointment), *Box of Tricks*, *Hollyoaks* (Lime Pictures), *Shameless* (Channel 4), *Take Me to Redcar* (BBC Radio 4).

Joe Dixon | Ajax

Trained at RADA. Associate Artist, Royal Shakespeare Company. First recipient of the Ian Charleson Best Actor Award.

Theatre includes: *The Orphan of Zhao, Boris Godunov, Troilus and Cressida* (RSC/The Wooster Group), *A Midsummer Night's Dream, Love's Labours Lost, Titus Andronicus,* Jacobethan Season – *The Malcontent, The Island Princess, The Roman Actor* (RSC, Olivier Award Outstanding Achievement. Olivier Award nominee, Best Supporting Actor), *The Winter's Tale* (National Theatre), *The Real Inspector Hound/The Critic* (Chichester Festival Theatre), *Cruel and Tende*r (Young Vic, Bouffes du Nord Vienna, Berlin, Chichester Festival Theatre), *Romeo and Juliet* (English Shakespeare Company, Young Vic), *Duchess of Malfi* (Wyndhams), *The Bacchae* (QEH South Bank), *As You Like It* (Cheek by Jowl, world tour), *The Father* (Belgrade Theatre), *Our Country's Good* (Gate Theatre, Dublin), *Morte D'Arthur* (Lyric Hammersmith) *Women Beware Women* (Royal Court).

Television includes: *Atlantis* (BBC), *Sirens, Dr Who, Criminal Justice, 32 Brinkburn Street, Silent Witness, Holding On, The Stretford Wives, When I'm Sixty Four.*

Film includes: *The Cold Light of Day, The Mummy Returns, The Changeling.*

Radio includes: *The Father, Arabian Nights, The Epic of Gilgamesh.*

Ben Karakashian | Stage Manager

Graduated from Royal Holloway University of London with BA Honours in Drama and Theatre Studies.

Stage management credits include *Moment of Truth, Tanzi Libre, Feathers in the Snow* (Southwark Playhouse), *Black Jesus, Soft of Her Palm , The Grand Duke , Goodnight Bird, Portraits, Perchance to Dream* (Finborough Theatre), *Quasimodo, Someone to Blame* (Kings Head Theatre), *The Folk Contraption* (Old Vic Tunnels and London Wonderground), *The Mikado* (Rosemary Branch Theatre and Kings Head Theatre), *Susanna's Secret* (Kings Head Theatre), *Trial by Jury and The zoo* (Rosemary Branch Theatre) *Beowulf: The Panto* (Rosemary Branch Theatre), *Pitch Perfect* (Tristan Bates Theatre).

Production management credits include *The Bunker Trilogy* (Southwark Playhouse). Assistant stage management credits include *Gatz: The Great Gatsby Uncut* (Noël Coward Theatre), *Exhibition Road Show Festival* (Exhibition Road; Dream).

James Kermack | Soldier

Theatre includes: *Fever Pitch* (national tour), *Animal Bordello* (Soho Theatre), *Guys and Dolls*, *Play It Again Sam* (Upstairs at the Gatehouse), *Saving Toad* (Pleasance), *A Thousand Miles of History* (Bussey Building), *Of Mice and Men* (National Tour), *The Crucible* (Wateryard), *Suburbia* (Pentameters Theatre), *Old Vic New Voices 24 Hour Plays* (Old Vic, 2006), *Pygmalion* (Old Vic/Theatre Royal Bath), *1 in 5* (Young Vic and Hampstead Theatre), *The Company Project: Playlist* (Arcola Theatre), *Kind Hearts and Coronets* (national tour), *Manor* (Tristan Bates Theatre), *Damaged* (Liverpool Everyman), *For Once I Was* (OVNV US/UK Exchange) and *Not Another Musical* (Look Left Look Right).

Film and TV includes: *The Lost* (Thamesgate Films), *Private Jenkins Is* (MOD/ Two Four Productions) and the Armed Forces award-winning *Don't Bottle It Up* campaign (BDA Creative). James also co-runs multi-award-nominated production company Nothin or Double Films www.nothinordoublefilms.com.

David Mercatali | Director

David is Associate Director at Southwark Playhouse. Previous credits at Southwark Playhouse are: Philip Ridley's *Tender Napalm*, for which he was nominated for the Evening Standard Outstanding Newcomer Award 2011, and *Feathers in the Snow*. Other credits include: Fringe First award winning *Dark Vanilla Jungle* (Pleasance, Edinburgh Fringe), *Black Jesus* (Finborough Theatre), *Someone to Blame* (King's Head Theatre), the premiere of Philip Ridley's *Moonfleece* (Riverside Studios and National Tour), *People's Day* (Pleasance, Islington), *Runners – the Return* (Underbelly, Edinburgh Fringe), *Weights* and his own play *The Sound* (Blue Elephant Theatre). He has also developed new work with Paines Plough, the Finborough and Theatre503.

Jordan Mifsud | Soldier

Trained at the American Academy of Dramatic Arts, New York, and the Royal Academy of Dramatic Art, graduating in 2012.

Theatre includes: *Moth* (HighTide/Bush Theatre) *55 Days* (Hampstead Theatre) and *The Two Worlds of Charlie F* (Theatre Royal Haymarket/ UK tour).

Training credits while at RADA include: *You Never Can Tell*, *From Both Hips*, *The House of Special Purpose*, *Twelfth Night* and *The Winter's Tale*.

Christopher Nairne | Lighting Design

Previous lighting designs for Supporting Wall include *Shallow Slumber* (Soho Theatre) and *The Jewish Wife* (Battersea Arts Centre). Previous shows at Southwark Playhouse include: *The Busy Body*, *Someone Who'll Watch Over Me* and *The Belle's Stratagem* (Red Handed Theatre Company), and *Henry V* (Southwark Playhouse Theatre Company).

Other recent theatre credits include: *Dracula* (for Theatre Royal Bath), *The School for Scandal* (Park Theatre and Theatre Royal Bury), *The Ghost Hunter* (Old Red Lion Theatre and UK tour), *Recording Hedda* (New Diorama Theatre), *Fiesta: The Sun Also Rises* and *Celebrity Night at Café Red* (Trafalgar Studios), *Boy in a Dress* (UK tour), *The Chicago Cowboy* (Rosemary Branch Theatre) and *A Dish of Tea with Dr Johnson* (Out of Joint, UK tour and Arts Theatre).

Opera work includes: *Vivienne* (Linbury Studio, Royal Opera House), *The Crocodile* (Riverside Studios), *La Bohème* (OperaUpClose; 2011 Olivier Award winner), *Albert Herring* (Surrey Opera) and *The Cunning Little Vixen* (Ryedale Festival Opera).

Cabaret work includes: numerous shows for acts such as Morgan & West, Frisky & Mannish, Shlomo and The Vocal Orchestra.

Further details and full credits available at www.christophernairne.co.uk

Max Pappenheim | Sound Design

Sound design and composition includes: *Black Jesus*, *Summer Day's Dream*, *The Hospital at the Time of the Revolution*, *Somersaults*, *The Soft of Her Palm*, *The Fear of Breathing* (Finborough Theatre); *CommonWealth* (Almeida Theatre); *Mrs Lowry and Son* (Trafalgar Studios); *Being Tommy Cooper* (UK Tour); *Borderland*, *Kafka v Kafka* (Brockley Jack Studio Theatre); *Four Corners One Heart* (Theatre503); *Freefall* (New Wimbledon Theatre Studio) and *Below the Belt* (Pleasance, Edinburgh). Directing includes: *Nothing is the End of the World*, *Perchance to Dream* (Finborough Theatre) and *Siegfried* (Fulham Opera). Nominated for Off West End Awards 2012 and 2013.

William Postlethwaite | Teucer

William graduated from LAMDA in 2011.

Theatre includes: *King Lear* (Bath Theatre Royal), *Longing* (Hampstead), *Cinderella The Midnight Princess* (Rose Theatre Kingston), *Collaborators* (National Theatre), *Fireface* (Young Vic), *As You Like It* (Royal Exchange Manchester).

Television includes: *The Suspicions of Mr Whicher*, *Midsomer Murders*.

Annie Rowe | Casting

Annie trained as an actress at the NYT and RADA before embarking on a career in casting in 2007. In 2011 she gained probabtionary membership of the Casting Directors' Guild of Great Britain.

Theatre credits include: *The Love Girl and the Innocent* (Southwark Playhouse), *Sex Cells* (Riverside Studios), *Economy Of Thought* (Assembly Rooms, Edinburgh), *The School for Scandal* (Park Theatre, 200/Theatre Royal Bury St Edmonds), *Yellow Face* (Park Theatre, 90), *The Duke in Darkness* (Tabard Theatre), *A Thousand Miles of History* (Bussey Building), *The Seagull* (Southwark Playhouse), *The Hotel Plays* (Grange Hotel), *Bee Detective* (Tin Bath Theatre Co), *The Art of Concealment* (Jermyn Street), *Fit and Proper People* (Soho Theatre/RSC), *Mr Happiness*, *The Water Engine* (Old Vic Tunnels), *Wife to James Whelan* (New Diorama), *Love on the Dole* (Finborough), *Alice Through the Looking Glass*, *Around the World in Eighty Days* (The Egg at Theatre Royal Bath), *Public Property* (Trafalgar Studios)

For Theatre503: *Meat*, *Man in the Middle*, *The Swallowing Dark* (with Liverpool Playhouse), *Sold*, *The Consultant*, *The Biting Point*, *The Charming Man*, *Breed*, *Epic*, *Wild Horses*, *Porn: The Musical*, *This Much Is True*, *Manorhouse*, *The Tin Horizon*.

Short films: *Rest Stop*, *Father's Day*, *Tough Guys*, *Waiting for Dawn*, *The Heart of Dicken Partridge*, *By Hook*, *Trailing Dirt*, *Modo and Mahu*.

Adam Riches | Odysseus

Adam is best known as a comedian, and won the Edinburgh Comedy Award 2011 for his show *Bring Me The Head of Adam Riches* (Pleasance Edinburgh and Soho Theatre London).

Theatre includes: *A Thousand Miles of History* (Bussey Building).

Television includes: *Crackanory*, *Common Ground*, *Cardinal Burns*, *A Touch of Frost*. Radio includes: *The Guns of Adam Riches* (BBC Radio 4).

John Schwab | Menelaos

Theatre includes: Man in *Special Delivery* (Time Wave Festival with Neil LaBute), Rocco Palmieri/Cameron Mackintosh in *Yellow Face* (Park Theatre), Mark in *The Leisure Society* (Trafalgar Studios), Saul Kimmer in *True West* (Sheffield Crucible), Mike in *Six Dance Lessons in Six Weeks* (understudied and played, Theatre Royal Haymarket), The Complete *Works of William Shakespeare* (*Abridg'd*), *The Complete History of America* (*Abridg'd*), The Complete Wod of God (*Abridg'd*) (Criterion Theatre), *Elvis the Musical*, (Piccadilly Theatre). John has also workshopped Ross

Howard's *No One Loves Us Here*, and directed the world premiere of David Spicer's theatrical debut, *Long Live the Mad Parade*.

Film and Television includes: *Zero Dark Thirty*, *The Fifth Estate*, *The Vatican*, *The Anomaly*, *Kick Ass 2*, *Jack Ryan*, *Nixon's the One*, *Episodes*, *The Special Relationship*, *Hotel Babylon*, *Ultimate Force*, *Monarch of the Glen*, *Doctor Who*, *The Only Boy for Me*, *Space Odyssey: A Voyage to the Planets*, *Make My Day*, *My Dad's the Prime Minister*, *Being Dom Joly* and *Hotel*.

Radio includes: *Book of the Week*, *Last Days of Detroit*, *Safety Catch*, *At Home in Mitford*, *The Stone Diaries*, *The Emigrants*, *A Life Story* and *The Grapes of Wrath*.

John is also an award-winning filmmaker and was nominated for a BIFA for his feature film producing debut *The Hide*.

Fiona Skinner | Soldier

Theatre includes: *My Imaginary Friend Patrick Stewart* (Theatre 503), Nabokov's *Brave New World* (Soho Theatre), *They May Not Mean To, But They Do* (The Bussey Building), *'AVE IT!* (Old Vic Tunnels), *People Like Us* (Vineyard Theatre), *Tell Me a Secret* (Southwark Playhouse), *Les Belles Soeurs* (Landor Theatre), *The Rimers of Eldritch* (Chelsea Theatre), *Market Boy* (Edinburgh Fringe Festival).

Television includes: *Call the Midwife* (Neal Street Productions/BBC), *Our Girl* (BBC) and three Episodes of *Doctors* (BBC).

Fiona was part of the Old Vic New Voices T.S Eliot Exchange (2011) and the 24-Hour Plays (2012). She was also nominated for the 2009 Spotlight Prize.

Supporting Wall | Producer

Producing company Supporting Wall was founded in 2008 by Ben Monks and Will Young. They have twice been nominated for the OffWestEnd Best Producer Award, in 2011 and 2012, and received a Stage One Bursary in 2010.

Recent productions include three world premieres with playwright Philip Ridley, including Edinburgh Fringe First Award winner *Dark Vanilla Jungle* (Royal Exchange Manchester/Edinburgh Fringe, 2013), the nationally-acclaimed *Tender Napalm* (Southwark Playhouse, 2011, UK tour, 2012) and his BNP-based drama *Moonfleece* (UK tour, 2010). They have also produced the world premiere of Chris Lee's social work drama *Shallow Slumber* (Soho Theatre, 2011), Danny Saleeb's chamber opera *Yellow* (Tête à Tête: The Opera Festival, 2011); JMK Award-winner *The Jewish Wife* (Battersea Arts Centre, 2010); and rapid-response political theatre event *Election Drama* (New Players Theatre,

2010), described by the *New Statesman* as 'a breathtaking feat of theatrical chutzpah'.

Supporting Wall has also managed and promoted UK and international tours for a range of clients across theatre, dance, comedy, film and festivals. For more information, visit www.supportingwall.com.

Karl Sydow | Producer

Future projects include *This May Hurt a Bit* by Stella Feehily, *Backbeat* on Broadway, *Our Country's Good* North American tour, *Under Milk Wood* directed by Terry Hands featuring Tony-winner Owen Teale, opening in Wales and NYC in Autumn 2013 to mark the centenary of Dylan Thomas's birth and the sixtieth anniversary of the premiere of *Under Milk Wood, The Last Confession* world tour featuring David Suchet and Brian Bedford.

Broadway credits include: *The Seagull* featuring Kristin Scott Thomas and Carey Mulligan; *All My Sons* with Katie Holmes; *American Buffalo* by David Mamet; *Our Country's Good* by Timberlake Wertenbaker (which received six Tony nominations, New York Critics Award Best Foreign Play, Olivier Award Best Play).

Other credits include: at BAM the NT's production of *Happy Days* by Samuel Beckett, featuring Fiona Shaw, directed by Deborah Warner; *Haunted* by Edna O'Brien featuring Brenda Blethyn; *Terra Haute* by Edmond White with Peter Eyre; *Backbeat* at the Royal Alexandra Theatre, Toronto, and at the Ahmanson Theatre in LA.

UK credits include *Our Country's Good* at the St James Theatre, London; *Backbeat* (Citizens Theatre, Glasgow, and Duke of York's Theatre, London); *Dish of Tea with Dr Johnson*, directed by Max Stafford-Clark; *The Line* by Timberlake Wertenbaker; *Memory* by Johnathan Lichtenstein, directed by Terry Hands; *Triptych* by Edna O'Brien; *Ring Round the Moon* by Jean Anouilh, adapted by Christopher Fry, directed by Sean Mathias at the Playhouse; *Jenufa* by Timberlake Wertenbaker, directed by Irina Brown at the Arcola Theatre; *Dirty Dancing* at the Aldwych Theatre, London, which achieved the largest advance sales in the history of the West End; the London and Sydney productions of *Dance of Death* with Sir Ian McKellen, Francis de la Tour and Owen Teale; *And Then There Were None* by Agatha Christie; *Bea Arthur at the Savoy, Auntie and Me*, with Alan Davies and Maggie Tyzack at Wyndhams; *Michael Moore, Live!* at the Roundhouse; the West End premiere of Noël Coward's *Semi Monde*; Kevin Elyot's *Mouth to Mouth* at the Albery Theatre, with Lyndsay Duncan and Michael Maloney; David Mamet's *Speed the Plow* with Mark Strong, Patrick Marber and Kimberly Williams; *Drummers* by Simon Bennet and *Some Explicit Polaroids* by Mark

Ravenhill (winner of the Evening Standard Award as Most Promising Newcomer), both directed by Max Stafford-Clark for Out of Joint; *Macbeth* with Rufus Sewell at the Queens Theatre; *A Swell Party*, a celebration of Cole Porter at the Vaudeville Theatre; Timberlake Wertenbaker's *Our Country's Good* (nominated for six Tony Awards and received the Olivier Award for Best Play and the New York Critics' Award for Best Foreign Play); *Hysteria* (Best Comedy, Olivier Awards); and an adaptation of Sue Townsend's novel *The Queen and I*, which was Out of Joint's inaugural production.

Karl was a founder member and continues to serve on the board of Out of Joint, the UK's leading producer of new writing for the theatre founded by Max Stafford-Clark after serving for thirteen years as Artistic Director of the Royal Court Theatre. Karl also served as a director of Renaissance Film Company. Renaissance productions have earned many awards including four Oscars from twelve nomination, and grossed a total box office in the UK and US of over \$100million. Renaissance Films include: *Henry V*, *Peter's Friends*, *Much Ado About Nothing*, *The Madness of King George*, *Twelfth Night* and *Wings of the Dove*.

He continues to act as an independent film and theatre producer. Projects with David Parfitt (his colleague from Renaissance and Oscar-winning producer for *Shakespeare in Love*), include *A Bunch of Amateurs* by Ian Hislop and Nick Newman featuring Burt Reynolds, Sir Derek Jacobi, Imelda Staunton and Samantha Bond; and *My Week with Marilyn*, featuring Michelle Williams, Eddie Redmayne, Sir Kenneth Branagh, Dominic Cooper, Emma Watson and Dame Judy Dench.

James Turner | Designer

James trained on the Motley Theatre Design Course and works as an assistant to Ultz, most recently on the West End production of *Mojo*.

Designs include*: Still Life/Red Peppers* (Old Red Lion), *Cuddles (*Oval House), *Cause Celebre* (Central School of Speech and Drama), *A Life* and *The Sluts of Sutton Drive* (Finborough), *I Am a Camera* and *Execution of Justice* (Southwark Playhouse), *Strong Arm* and *That Moment* (Underbelly, Edinburgh), *Mercury Fur* (Trafalgar Studios and Old Red Lion), *The Fire Raisers, Oh What a Lovely War* and *Much Ado About Nothing* (British American Drama Academy), *Thrill Me* (Tristan Bates and Charing Cross Theatre), *Plain Jane* (Royal Exchange Studio, Manchester), *No Wonder* (Library Theatre, Manchester) and *A Man of No Importance* (Union Theatre and Arts Theatre).

Upcoming work includes: being Associate Designer on *A View from the Bridge* at the Young Vic. James won the 2013 Off-West-End Award for Best Set Designer for *Mercury Fur*.

Timberlake Wertenbaker | Playwright

Timberlake Wertenbaker grew up in the Basque Country and lives in London. Her plays include *Our Country's Good*, *The Grace of Mary Traverse*, *Three Birds Alighting on a Field*, *The Break of Day* and *Credible Witness* (for the Royal Court), *The Love of the Nightingale* (Royal Shakespeare Company), *Galileo's Daughter* (Theatre Royal, Bath), *The Ash Girl* (Birmingham Rep), *After Darwin* (Hampstead Theatre) and *The Line* (Arcola Theatre). Her translations and adaptations include Sophocles' *Theban Plays*, Mnouchkine's *Mephisto* (for the RSC), Euripides' *Hecuba* (ACT, San Francisco), Eduardo de Filippo's *Filumena* (Piccadilly), Anouilh's *Wild Orchids* (Chichester Festival Theatre), Gabriela Preissova's *Jenufa* (Arcola), Sophocles' *Elektra* (Getty), Racine's *Phèdre* (Shakespeare Festival, Stratford, Ontario) and Racine's *Britannicus* (Wilton's Music Hall).

Opera includes: *The Love of the Nightingale*, music by Richard Mills (Perth International Arts Festival and Sydney Opera House).

TV/Film productions include *The Children*, starring Kim Novak and Ben Kingsley, and *Do Not Disturb*, starring Frances Barber. Recent radio work includes: *The Memory of Gold* (BBC Radio 3), an adaptation of A. S. Byatt novel *Possession* for BBC Radio Woman's Hour and Tolstoy's *War and Peace* for the BBC in 2014.

Timberlake is the recipient of numerous awards including an Olivier Award and the 1990 New York Drama Critics Award for *Our Country's Good* and a Writers' Guild Award for *Three Birds Alighting on a Field*. She is currently joint Artistic Director of Natural Perspective and the Chair in Playwriting at the University of East Anglia.

Douglas Wood | Child

Douglas is seventeen, and has performed in many roles both in and out of school. He has taken part in the RSC's production of *A Midsummer Night's Dream*, in which he was Robin. As well as being a member of the National Youth Theatre, he also played Benedict in Shakespeare's *Much Ado About Nothing*. In the past he was involved in Timberlake Wertenblake's translation of *Antigone*, performed at Southwark Playhouse. In addition he has founded a theatre company called The Innocence who to date have had two highly successful productions, the most recent being the sold-out *The Innocence*, which he wrote and starred. He has appeared in many plays at Southwark Playhouse, and is a part of their Young Company.

Southwark Playhouse Theatre Company was founded in 1993 by Juliet Alderdice, Tom Wilson and Mehmet Ergen. They identified the need for a high quality accessible theatre which would provide opportunities for the best emerging companies and practitioners, and also act as a major resource for the local community. They leased a disused workshop in a then comparatively neglected part of Southwark and turned it into a flexible theatre space.

The theatre quickly put down strong roots in Southwark, developing an innovative, free-at-source, education programme. It has worked closely with teachers, Southwark Borough Council, businesses and government agencies to improve educational achievement and raise aspirations.

In 2007 it moved to its second premises in arches beneath Platform 1 of London Bridge Station where it was home to a 150-seat studio theatre and a second performance space, The Vault, which served as a platform for developing and nurturing cutting edge theatre. At the beginning of 2013 the theatre vacated these arches to make way for the redevelopment of London Bridge Station. Its third home, on Newington Causeway, will provide a temporary home for the theatre until the station is completed in 2018.

Over the past twenty years Southwark Playhouse has established itself as one of London's leading studio theatres, representing high quality work by new and emerging theatre practitioners. Under successive talented artistic directors, Mehmet Ergen (now Artistic Director of the Arcola Theatre), Erica Whyman (now Deputy Artistic Director of the Royal Shakespeare Company), Thea Sharrock (who recently directed *The Bodyguard* at the Adelphi Theatre and *Cause Célèbre* at the Old Vic), Gareth Machin (now Artistic Director of Salisbury Playhouse) and Ellie Jones, it has become an indispensable part of theatre in London. Under the current Artistic Directorship of Chris Smyrnios, the theatre has won multiple awards including the Off West End Theatre Award for Special Achievement (2013) and the Peter Brook Empty Space Award (2011).

Staff List

For more information about the forthcoming season in our new home and to book tickets visit

ww.southwarkplayhouse.co.uk

You can also support us online by joining our Facebook (search for 'Southwark Playhouse') and Twitter (@swkplay) pages

Our Ajax

Timberlake Wertenbaker grew up in the Basque Country and lives in London. Her plays include *Our Country's Good*, *The Grace of Mary Traverse*, *Three Birds Alighting on a Field*, *The Break of Day* and *Credible Witness* (all for the Royal Court), *The Love of the Nightingale* (RSC), *Galileo's Daughter* (Theatre Royal, Bath), *The Ash Girl* (Birmingham Rep), *After Darwin* (Hampstead Theatre) and *The Line* (Arcola Theatre). Her translations and adaptations include Sophocles' *Theban Plays* (RSC), Euripides' *Hecuba* (ACT, San Francisco), Eduardo de Filippo's *Filumena* (Piccadilly), Gabriela Preissova's *Jenufa* (Arcola), Sophocles' *Elektra* (Getty), Racine's *Phèdre* (Shakespeare Festival, Stratford, Ontario) and Racine's *Britannicus* (Wilton's Music Hall). Opera includes *The Love of the Nightingale*, music by Richard Mills (Perth International Arts Festival and Sydney Opera House). Radio includes *Dianeira*, *The Memory of Gold* and an adaptation of A. S. Byatt's *Possession*. Timberlake is joint Artistic Director of Natural Perspective and Chair in Playwriting at the University of East Anglia.

TIMBERLAKE WERTENBAKER

Our Ajax

FABER & FABER

First published in 2013
by Faber and Faber Limited
74–77 Great Russell Street
London WC1B 3DA

Typeset by Country Setting, Kingsdown, Kent CT14 8ES
Printed and bound by CPI Group (UK) Ltd, Croydon CR0 4YY

A CIP record for this book
is available from the British Library

ISBN 978-0-571-31346-4

2 4 6 8 10 9 7 5 3

Introduction

I remember the British-Guyanese poet and playwright Fred D'Aguiar once saying that when he went into his room to write he was not aware of his colour or of his gender. The writing mind follows other identifications.

I'm not too keen on violence, I've joined many anti-war demonstrations, I like flowers, I understand what it is to be a woman in the twenty-first century.

My writing mind wanted to go elsewhere. To a play that was mostly about men. And war.

Soldiers don't choose wars, the politicians do that. I was interested in exploring what draws people into the army. I was fascinated by military leaders, the idea of command.

I had been intrigued for some time by Sophocles' play *Ajax* but I found it hard to read. I asked my friend the Greek scholar Margaret Williamson if she would help me translate it as we'd already worked together on several Greek plays. We spent three weeks in the Basque Country, deep in dictionaries, fed by kind friends.

When I translate, I usually start with a literal and then make it less literal as I go along. However, I always try to stay close to the original text. I knew immediately this wouldn't happen here. A new play was superimposing itself on the literal: contemporary, based on current wars, set in a British army base. The war in Afghanistan was dragging on and there were a lot of headlines about casualties – and suicides. *Ajax* became *Our Ajax*.

Purni Morell, then the head of the National Theatre Studio, offered me one of their writing cells and we started interviewing people. We contacted an organisation called Veterans in Prison. This led us to Danny McEneany in

Liverpool, a squaddie who'd spent some time in prison. He was open, honest. He really liked the idea that there was a Greek origin to the play I was writing. Soldiers, however disaffected, feel strongly about their historical links. Purni directed a reading with a fabulous cast. I owe them all thanks.

Many people spoke to me during and after that time. Experts on military history and Combat-Related Post-Traumatic Stress Disorder, soldiers, a Regimental Sergeant Major and Commanding Officers. I was led to Jonathan Shay's fascinating book, *Achilles in Vietnam*, Patrick Hennessey's hilarious *The Junior Officers' Reading Club* and Freud's 'Rat Man'. I watched endless war films and documentaries, in particular the extraordinary *Restrepo* by the much-missed Tim Hetherington, who died in Libya in 2011. The writing mind is ravenous. You take what you can to portray what you can. You make no judgements.

And there is always the family. Even over a Christmas dinner, the mind watches. I have military cousins and my stepson joined the Gurkhas.

I was invited to Toronto by Peggy Shannon of Ryerson University for their project Women and War. A female colonel from the Israeli army was especially illuminating.

I've had very generous help from many quarters in gathering information for this play, including from the current cast. Whatever truth it has I owe to others, but if I may paraphrase my Ajax, 'any fucking mistakes, they're fucking mine'.

Timberlake Wertenbaker
October 2013

Characters

Our Ajax was inspired by Sophocles' *Ajax*
and borrows freely from it.

OUR AJAX

Before dawn.
A solitary man with a rifle herding a troupe of
imaginary prisoners who happen to be sheep, goats,
donkeys and a cow.

Ajax
　　Ara ha ra wah.
　　Greetings God,
　　are you there?
　　I got body count body count –
　　look at this:
　　fucking dead most of 'em.
　　And these my prisoners.

　　He hits out.

　　A little enhanced interrogation
　　hah wra.

　　He kicks, slams a head.

　　Foxy beast I know your tricks:
　　Odysseus trying to slip away
　　toupitripton: you're not going to die just yet.
　　Bag on head, spreadeagled on the floor
　　blood oozing
　　bucket full of rats to eat your windy asshole
　　cos that's what you are a windy asshole thief
　　and what you're gonna confess under water
　　is how you took what was mine by right.

　　Threatens.

　　Wrah!

Don't tell me to have pity Godgirl.
Didn't they humiliate me? And my men?
Was that right, was that right?
I'll obey you in everything else, yes ma'am
cos you love me and I love you
now I squashed those motherfucking maggots,
got my honour back.
Move, animals!

He marches out.

Odysseus, forensic. Athena emerges and watches.

Athena
Hey.
Hey there.
What are you doing there
on all fours
sniffing the ground like a hound?
Right by his tent too.
The man's blown up:
God's IED.
Come over here,
I've lots to tell you.

Odysseus
Athena . . .
I love your voice:
the sound of reveille
bugling through
the morning air.

Athena
For your ears only
though.
Here.

Odysseus
Where? I can't see you.
Only your voice

reverberates.
God's signals transmitting –
I receive clearly, see no one.

Athena

Here – sit here and
so, tell me.

Odysseus

Carnage in the camp.

Athena

I can see that.
This is an intelligence test
military.
Facts. Deduction. Strategy.

Odysseus

First our sniffer dogs
trained for years
to detect explosives.
Throats slit –
some raging hand.
Then the herds, goats, sheep
of the training village.

Athena

Your little theatre
of war.

Odysseus

Well, it was my idea:
pretend first so when you do it for real –

Athena

it doesn't feel real. I love the human mind.

Odysseus

We call it training. Local colour. Know what to expect –
I thought it was your idea –
I heard your voice –

Athena
    – in your mind.

Odysseus
    So the herds shot,
    death blossom,
    the only source of fresh meat
    source of pride and wealth
    to the people here.
    And the men guarding the herds
    ambushed
    – only for real.
    Not a way to make local friends.
    A figure was seen
    bounding over the walls
    blood scattered like breadcrumbs.
    I follow the tracks.
    They lead here.
    But some things don't make sense.

Athena
    That's why I'm here.
    I'm the figure
    that makes things clear
    puts them into words
    you understand.
    Concepts easy on the human mind
    like war. Enemy. Win.
    So I'm the goddess of war.

Odysseus
    And wisdom. That's what I need right now.

Athena
    I'm good at wisdom: might is right.
    Simple concise and irrefutable.
    And don't offend the gods:
    warning to the wise.

Odysseus

Have I sniffed the right man?

Athena

He's the one who did it.

Odysseus

Wasn't it a bit irrational?

Athena

Another human word
bound by the physical limitations
of the point of view.
He didn't get the honour he deserved.
A soldier will fight long and hard for some leaves
    on his head,
a bit of coloured ribbon on his chest
but what happens when he doesn't get them?
Even gods want recognition. Especially gods.
Remember that.
But more important,
where's his promotion, General Odysseus?

Odysseus

I was only made Brigadier.

Athena

Only a matter of time. They can't skip all the ranks
    at once.

Odysseus

If the Lieutenant Colonel feels passed over
why take it out on dogs and goats?

Athena

He thought he was plunging his hands into your carcass.

Odysseus

I've been called foxy. Bovine
would describe him more than me.

Athena

You'd be meat if I hadn't prevented it.
He was creeping up to the Generals' quarters.
You were next.

Odysseus

What stopped him?

Athena

Me. I
scrambled his eyes, his brains and drew him to the
    cattle
who rustled and snorted and grunted
well, I can't always tell the difference myself.
Then to the dogs snoring
twitching in dreams of sniff and chase,
just like you, Odysseus.
And as his mind wandered and
stepped on all the unexploded mines of terror,
I launched a barrage of blood-soaked memories
again and again like mortars in his eyes.
He didn't know where he was.
Past horror crashed into the present
neon flashes of mutilation
and children, that always works,
on, off, the same again and again,
his own, a film, a story, who knows?
As I said,
scrambled.
Want to watch?
I'll call him.

Odysseus

Not out here!
He's dangerous even when he's sane.

Athena

Afraid?

Odysseus

You told me yourself:
never interrupt your enemy when he's making a mistake.
Let him stay inside.

Athena

You enjoy laughing at your enemies.

Odysseus

I can laugh at him from a distance.

Athena

Don't you want a front-row view?
See what a god can do.

Odysseus

I think I know.

Athena

He thinks I love him.
All men think God loves them
and speaks to them.
Sometimes they're right.

Odysseus

How can we know for sure?

Athena

That's just it: you can't.
Here come his men.
Wear this. Camouflage.

Odysseus

That's sheepskin.

Athena

That's what I said. Camouflage. Won't be the last time
you get out of a scrape with sheep's camouflage
and you'll take credit for the idea.
You know what can be hidden under the belly of a
    four-footed animal.

Odysseus

That donkey that came towards the gate,
explosives attached to its belly –
it was Ajax who sensed danger.
He can smell an explosive a mile off.
He ran towards it, chased it away from the men
put his own life at risk, always does.

Athena

Sometimes I envy the excitement of being human,
all that life and death stuff. You have to be human
  to be brave.

Odysseus

Has his courage run out? I can't imagine.

Athena

Was there ever a man with more foresight in action?
Did the right thing at the right time.
Man of few words, heart full of courage.
See how one day can turn things around?

Odysseus

But how did it happen? Why?

Athena

A challenge for your human brain.
Just remember, Odysseus,
we don't like it when you go around thinking you're
  gods.
Modesty, even false, suits men well.
Now put on this clothing and act like a sheep.

Athena and Odysseus stay onstage.

Ajax's men come on.

Soldier

So I have this dream
I'm running through a bunch of street markets
I'm alone cos

I've been cut off from my platoon
I'm trying to find my way back to the guys
it's just me and nobody else
running.
What am I supposed to do?
I'm scared shitless.

Soldier

I see battlefields
I'm running away
I fall down and shoot
people are running and screaming
I hear grenades, bullets and a voice
take care of my kids.

Soldier

I see these friends
then I notice it's just their heads.
I've lined them up
and they're talking to me.

Soldier

And this brass says,
this perfumed prince
a real seven-thousand-mile screwdriver
he says:
you're lacking in moral fibre.
And they shoot me:
firing squad.

CSM

OK. As you were.
Any flashbacks?

Soldier

Yessir.

CSM

Persistent?

Soldier
Yessir.

CSM
Out with it.

Soldier
Yessir. Penelope Cruz
in that movie
naked.

CSM
I mean battlefield flashbacks, where you've been
I'm looking for trauma here
not your sex life.

Soldier
I was there
with her
I keep seeing her.

Soldier
Isn't Odysseus' wife called Penelope?

Soldier (*sings sotto voce*)
'I don't know but I've been told
Penelope's pussy's mighty cold –'

CSM
I'm not fucking interested in Penelope's fucking pussy!
Any recurring action?

Soldier
My girlfriend, my girlfriend, my girlfriend, recurring.

CSM
OK. As you were.

Soldier
Situation normal all fucked-up.

CSM
Press-up position now. Down!

Soldier

But –

Soldier

What about Ajax?

CSM

Lieutenant Colonel A. Ajax to you.

Soldier

Yeah. Ajax. Our Ajax.
There's these rumours.

CSM

Of course there are rumours, this is the army.

Soldier

Persistent rumours.

Soldier

Recurring memories rumours.

Soldier

Flashback in the night:
someone killed the dogs.

CSM

Wouldn't be one of ours. We like dogs. Maybe some
ANA on dope.

Soldier

And Odysseus saying –

Soldier

Brigadier Odysseus saying –

Soldier

That bastard Odysseus spreading rumours because
he hates Ajax and us.

Soldier

Always been jealous –

Soldier

I thought I saw him sneaking around the tent –

Soldier

Muttering to himself.

Soldier

I think he prays.

They laugh.

Odysseus (*to Athena*)

I'll get those fucking bastards sent on a suicide mission.

Athena

Shut up. Stick to being a sheep.

Soldier

I heard something.

CSM

A sheep bleating. Proves nothing's happened.

Soldier

There's usually more sheep –

Soldier

And Ajax – he's been very quiet.

CSM

The Colonel never speaks, prefers to act.

Soldier

We haven't seen him this morning.

Soldier

He usually comes out. Makes a joke. It's not funny
    but we laugh anyway,
because we're happy to see him. Our Ajax.

Soldier

He still hasn't come out.

Soldier

Maybe you could go see him?

Because if there's some truth
and he's the one with the nightmares
what are we going to do?

CSM
He is the best of our COs

Soldier
the most solid

Soldier
always looks after his men

Soldier
always does what's right

Soldier
knows the enemy

CSM
so nothing can be wrong. Not with Colonel Ajax.

Soldiers
Ajax!

Odysseus (*to Athena*)
I wish my men spoke of me like that.

Athena
I wish I was the goddess of love. But I'm the goddess
of war. You're Odysseus, the Brigadier with brains.
It's more effective to be feared than loved.

Odysseus
Men will do anything for Ajax.

Athena
I said effective.

Soldier
There's Tecmessa!

Odysseus

And he even gets the beautiful female medic. She
arrives, her eyes pass over me, one glance at him,
that's it. Aren't women supposed to prefer brain
to brawn?

Athena

Tecmessa!
I forgot about her.
She could ruin everything
bring Ajax back to his senses.
And I can't get inside her head:
she hears different voices.
I hate having women in the army.
Let's go: look like a sheep who's just seen his flock.

Odysseus

How do I do that?

Athena

Use your imagination. I think you call it empathy.

Athena leaves. Odysseus trots after her.

Tecmessa comes on.

Tecmessa

Help me!
Your great, your mighty, your strong
tautly muscled brave giant
your Ajax
lies stricken, slack.
Disease, disorder, some trauma, I don't know.
I understand bodies, mend what I can.
Bodies are the same everywhere
but the anatomy of a soldier's mind
however trained and twisted into shape
follows no pattern I know.
Ajax's soul belongs to his men.
Help him.

Soldier

So the rumours –

Soldier

It's very quick:
everything's normal
usual stuff
and then one day
crack and thump
darkness breaks loose.
World War Three enemy alarm clock.

CSM

I've seen it before
the man's out there
really out there
or
you look at the man
and the bank of courage
is empty. Nothing left.

Soldier

But not Ajax –
never Colonel Ajax.
A man like Ajax doesn't crack.

CSM

Tecmessa:
You've saved our limbs,
you've diagnosed our pain,
you always speak with knowledge.
Tell us.

Tecmessa

No knowledge in any book
to diagnose what's happened to this man.
Some mania in the night
seized him
undid his senses.

You can see the result in the tent:
hacked pieces, bloody meat strewn all over
dogs' heads, and hear the bleating
the sacrificial victims of his hands,
the butchery
of his rage.

Soldier

It's the same news.
We can't escape now
the rumour that's been spreading through the camp.

Soldier

What will they do to him
if they know for sure?

Soldier

If he's destroyed the dogs,
trained for years, source of our safety,
and the goats, source of food for the villages,
what will happen to all of us?

Soldier

What do we do?

Soldier

What fiendish alien jumped on him from behind?

Soldier

A fire of rage in the pit of his stomach burning out
 of control? I had it once, fired sixty rounds at nothing.

CSM

Hard to imagine anything like that with Colonel Ajax –
who doesn't even turn his head at a mortar attack.

Soldier

What happened? Chronologically?

CSM

When a man breaks

he's already lost the chronology –
but give us the events anyway.

Tecmessa
It was the middle of the night
when in my culture we pray because at that time
the blood-soaked earth releases the stench
of death and the damp fumes of pain sweep
over those who remain.
And so I was awake.
He dressed to go out
full combat gear, took hold of his weapons.
I asked him:
what are you doing, Ajax?
You haven't been summoned
no calls, no trumpet or siren
no mortar attack, no rockets, not even a hand grenade,
    no sniper, no panic –
it's all calm out there
and the men are asleep.
He didn't say anything
but the look on his face demanded silence.
There is a place in men's minds where women can't go.
Same in any culture
any side of war any time
this veil over words.
I watched him rush out.
What happened then I can't say
but he comes back
as a sliver of dawn cracks open the night
drenched in blood and
leading his woolly prisoners
lots of them – sheep, goats, even a cow.
He starts cutting the throats of some
and others, with his own arms,
pulls off their heads, breaks their spines –
he torments others as if they're men

lunging forward to terrify
stepping back
insults, taunts
bags over their heads
laughing at the two Generals
Menelaos, Agamemnon
and at Odysseus
mocking that now they were even
and they'd all got what was coming to them.
He takes a plank, a bucket of water,
ties down a sheep
and pours water down its nose.
And curses I'd never heard before
even in this army.
A new language of rage.

And then very slowly he begins to calm down
and he looks around the room.
The wreckage.
And seeing the piles of dead animals
legs and heads thrown around, the smell
and those still tied,
he crumbles
cries out, hits his head
and then for a long time sits speechless.
Then he turns to me,
sees the events flickering in my eyes
even if I try to turn off the movie
and insists I tell him exactly what happened.
So I tell him
exactly what happened
the way I tell a kid
he's just lost an arm, both legs
but quickly I say
false limbs, replacement, you almost can't tell the
    difference –
look at those guys who cycle –

try for the Paralympics –
but not sure what to say now
about the mind. A prosthetic mind?
Retrain his memories? So I stop.
And he starts mewling in a way I've never heard before.
Because you know Ajax
and he's always said
that crying and snivelling are for the weak –
those with no spirit or guts, the fobbits
who try never to leave the camp
shirk patrol and the only sound you'd ever hear
   from him
was a bellow louder than a bull's.
But now he's wailing, shrill whining,
his voice a thinning reed
as he lies prostrate
in the middle of the cadavers:
everything he's hacked to pieces.
But what I hear through the moans and laments
is that he's planning something.
Now please, come and help.
He could be won over
by the comforting sound
of combat mates, the chorus of his battles
echoing what he is, what he was.
Help me.

Soldier

   Who's going in?
   I'd rather face the Terries
   than Ajax in a fury.

Ajax (*off*)

   Whoa whoa woe.

Tecmessa

   Do you hear him?

Howls his pain like a dog to the moon
or raped victim crying to the dawn

Ajax
IO WHOA.

Soldier
What memory in his mind
has come back to bite him, rabid?

Ajax
The child.
Where's my child?

Tecmessa
I sent the child away
at dawn – told him to find a woman any woman
clerical staff combat service support
told him to say nothing.
Woe to me if he calls him now.

Ajax
Where's my brother? Where's Teucer?
Teucer should be back now.

CSM
He's making some sense.
Might be good for him to see us now.

Tecmessa
I'll open the tent
you can see what he's done,
what he's come to.

Ajax
Io.

Ajax in the middle of bloody carcasses. He sees the men.

Men,
bound to me in loyalty

look:
red waves crashed around me
in a perfect storm of murder.

Tecmessa
Talk to him.
Words can soothe a shattered mind.

Silence.

Ajax
Yo!
Men.
Mates.
We've been on patrol together:
you know what happens
when you step on a mine
limbs fly through the air
in bits – up – and hang there –
sometimes a sniper
unseen close range
the jaw flies off
and you know what you have to do.
Only you can save me now.
See this brain split open – crack –
grey matter spilling out
oozes down my legs,
see this mutilation
of the mind.
Come here
and finish me.
Kill me.
Now.

CSM
Colonel Ajax –

Ajax
Ajax?

Look at the brave, the battle hardened, the lionhearted,
  the great and strong-muscled hero.
Look how I've distinguished myself in arm-to-arm
  combat with the enemy.
Look at the tame, four-footed, trusting enemy
  combatants I mowed down,
some with my bare hands too.
Some boondoggle.
Hilarious yo
I've been cut down to size all right
cut down to nothing. Crazy. Dinky dau. Fugazi
Get out! Hot foot it back to your pastures.
All of you out! Aiai.

CSM

Colonel, for God's sake, come back to your senses.

Ajax

And I let those cursed sons of bitches slip through
  my hands
and that slime fox medal-stealing shiny-assed Brigadier
  Odysseus –
instead I killed this brave army with their helmets of
  spiralling horns.
Look at these battle-hardened herds of goats bac bac
leaving their blood trail
how I've won their hearts and minds.

CSM

It's done, it can't be undone –
but if it's kept quiet –

Soldier

Say it's a rumour – snuff it out –

Soldier

Contain it: we know you well
we can follow your orders
even without orders.

Ajax (*over*)

    Io.
I can feel your eyes on me
instrument of my doom.
Yes you, Odysseus
the man with the bag of finely ground words
trickling through the camp.
Erasing everything my men did
with your brain tricks –
sucking up to the Generals
and stealing my reputation.
And now you lead the laughter
whip it up with your baton
the cymbal clang of jokes, the drumming of my shame
shame shame shame shame.

Soldier

    We won't allow that, Ajax.

Ajax

    If only I could get my hands on him now
even if I'm a wreck
send those rats up his ass
hosepipe down his nose.

CSM

    Steady there – Ajax –
Can't you see the trouble you're in?

Ajax

    Kill that slippery piece of shit-hate
then the Generals and at last, kill myself.
Ajax.
K.I.A.
The end.

Tecmessa

    Wish for this and then wish for our death as well.
What will happen to us if you die?

Ajax

    A god's voice of war
    I heard it clearly:
    kill them! kill them all!
    Guiding my steps in the dark
    I felt the god's love, the god's command:
    there's the sniper over there,
    lying in the dark. Got one of your men. Shoot!
    That child's not holding a ball:
    it's a hand grenade.
    There over the wall see those shadows?
    Here take these light intensifying night-vision binoculars
    and you'll see the Terries. Knock down that door,
        quick, shoot –
    quick, mortars coming from over there,
    hear the scream? One of yours again –
    I wanted to hurt, I wanted to hurt, I wanted to hurt –
    but it was sheep all the time. Or one of the dogs
    who saved my leg the other day. Sorry, dog: friendly fire
    this motherfucking mother of all fucking battles was
        a fucking mistake.

Tecmessa

    He was once so solid:
    I know: some used to whisper-thick.
    and now to say these things –

Ajax

    The contours of hell –
    the burning flesh – smell of cordite – the sound
    toc toc toc mortars – listen.
    Take me, take me now
    down far down – I'm not staying here:
    not with these eyes on me:
    the whole army watching –
    dig the dust with my own hands, hide underground,
        quick.

Tecmessa (*to the Soldiers*)
Can't you do anything?

Soldier
How many times
have we restrained a mate physically
when it got rough – easy.
But our Colonel? Ajax? Can't.

Tecmessa
Speak to him then!

Soldier
Sir –

Ajax
Months then years stuck here.
Dust seeps into the mind,
blood spatters on the retina.
No R and R for Ajax now.
But let me tell you:
this place has never seen someone like me before.
Over now.
Fade out.

Soldier
You're a legend,
legends don't fade.
Stories of your bravery,
we tell them every night.

Ajax
When my father fought here
he always got the medals
and the promotion.
When he went home
in triumph:
there on his breast,
puffed out like bright plumage,
the multicoloured glory of

decorations
and the beat of silence before his name.
RESPECT.
But here I am
his son in the same place and with the same strength
just as brave and done as much
but I've been passed over.
Passed over always
dishonoured.
Those two Generals
promoted Odysseus above me.
He's the Brigadier
commands the men
next stop General.
Name on every list:
first of the top third.
And where's Ajax?
I've got nothing to show for what I've done here.
They ignored all that Ajax did –
But if I my mind hadn't gone AWOL
thrown this illness on me
this cloak of martial fury
making me soak my hands in goat blood
up to my elbows in sheepshit –
so now they can all laugh at me.

God hates me
the army despises me
and this Asian desert
finds me repellent.
Now what?

Tecmessa

Ajax . . .

Ajax

Get sent home?
And how do I appear before my father?

36

I stand there and he looks at me
and I've got nothing
no badge of courage
no medal no promotion nothing
to prove I've even fucking been here.
How am I supposed to face him?
There has to be some way
I can show my father I'm his son.
Maybe I could take on the enemy by myself,
blow up a few before I die
hold a compound on my own
but those Generals would be only too pleased,
say it was a planned operation
and take the credit.
So I'm not doing that.

Tecmessa
Ajax.

Ajax
It'd be a crying shame
to try to stick to life
when this life is just
a big bag of dicks.
I don't have time for a man
who drags himself over the scorched earth
of empty hope.
A real man
doesn't go crawling low on his belly:
he either lives well
or dies well. Mess up the first,
that leaves the second.
Orders from above.

Tecmessa
Ajax,
it is the fate imposed upon them
that men find hardest to bear –

Ajax

    I was prepared to return home without a limb
    without a life even but not
    without honour –
    you have the Military Cross – what can you know
        about anger?

Tecmessa

    I was born in a land that was troubled, strong and
        proud
    decimated by your army.
    My father, my brothers, my cousins, you got them all.
    And then, for what? In a casual flourish of fire power
    my mother and a sister
    smothered by the mantle of one bomb
    sent to the wrong place:
    collateral damage of your force
    but even too much for you.
    Death, life, suicide, survival, the straws look the same.
    I picked the one that ordered survival.
    An orphan child,
    treated, bandaged, sent with another sister to your
        country
    to be collaterally undamaged,
    a bandage on your nation's guilt.

Ajax

    Tecmessa, I know your background.

Tecmessa

    But not my mind –
    what I couldn't tell you.
    How fixed in that mind
    was the memory of limbs
    scattered to the corners of the room,
    and fixed in my heart
    the desire to put the pieces back.
    In my dreams, recurring,

I stitched back to life
the jigsaw of the bodies I had lost.
And then, any life, anyone, anywhere.
How to do this?
Where else but in another war?
And since I needed other brothers fathers cousins
where else but here in this army –
yours since you were now my country?
And I begged to come out here.
Listen Ajax, listen carefully. My first day:
there you were.
Not like the others, apart, bigger, Ajax.
No need for words because your famous nose
for IEDs never missed the moments I might explode.
And you cradled me, father brother friend and lover
and all anger subsided in your arms.
Don't abandon me, not now
because the day you decide to die
what will happen to me?
To our child?
Your own son?
We have no home but you Ajax.

Ajax (*to Tecmessa*)
Remember the day
you clambered out of the TAV
on to the turret
no thought of the sniper fire
bullets smashing into the metal
inches from your legs.
Saved two of my men,
dragging them to safety.
Held the third in your arms
a sweet tender breath in death.
You didn't flinch then.
Don't flinch now.

Tecmessa
Remember then
the sweet attention I gave you
in your loneliness, in my pain.
I gave you the jewels in my tears
the breeze of hope in my despair
forgetfulness of past violence.
Remember the soothing warmth of our nights
the joyful peace in our war
the enemy's loving hand –
and remember that a man without gratitude
who forgets the delicate breath
of tenderness
foregoes his greatness.
Where's the honour, the manhood
in having no memory?

CSM
We respect her and you might respect what she says.

Ajax
I've always respected her
but she has to do what I ask.

Tecmessa
Haven't I always done what you asked of me?

Ajax
Yes, sometimes even before I asked.

A beat between them.

Bring me my son so I can see him.

Tecmessa
I sent him away.
I was afraid you would kill him.

Ajax
But now
I want to speak to him.

Tecmessa

He's with other children. A nightmare
fixed in his mind.

Ajax

I know about nightmares. Don't keep him from me.
What are you waiting for?

Tecmessa (*to the CSM*)

Would you – please?

The CSM leaves.

Ajax

What did he see?

Tecmessa

I don't know what he saw –
perhaps he doesn't either –

Ajax

But you think I am still –
that what he'll see
is the face in his nightmare?

Tecmessa

No.
You are Ajax.
You will always be Ajax.

Ajax

Ajax never harmed a child –
did he?

The Boy comes on.

A child with wide open eyes
in the corner of the room . . .

Tecmessa

Ajax? . . .

Ajax (*coming to*)

Come here, son, come into my arms.
If he really is my son,
these corpses won't bother him.
Time you were bloodied
and learned to carry your pack
on the mined road of combat.
Get him used
to the ways of his father.
Child, may you find on your path better luck than
   your father
but in all other ways may you be like your father
and then you won't have been born for nothing.
But I envy you now because you have no sense
of the harm coming your way.
Life is sweet before we're conscious –
until we're scorched by joy and sorrow.
You'll have to show your father's enemies
the kind of man you are –
but not yet – not yet –
No – until then –
feed on the sweet breezes of the air,
let your spirit dance lightly
to the beat of your mother's joy.
No man not a single one of them
will dare insult you when I'm gone.
I'm leaving you both in the care of my brother Teucer –
Where is he? Why isn't he here yet?
He'll be the sound guardian of your youth.
Guide your steps into manhood –
Now, son, take this weapon, look, hold it like this.
This will be for you.
SA80A2, accurate: look at the length of the barrel.
But keep it clean or it jams.
You dismantle it like this.
Learn to maintain it – clean and oil. Always keep it clean.

This is yours, your rifle, your luck.
Now: strike, seize, grasp.
Tecmessa, don't make a public spectacle of yourself
  by weeping.
Let's go into the tent
before I end up on YouTube.

Soldier
We don't like this

CSM
the possible meaning of these words

Soldier
we know every detail of his face but we've never seen
  that look

Soldier
empty.

Soldier
What are we going to do?

Tecmessa
Ajax, what are you going to do?

Ajax
Don't ask for details
you know I don't like them.

Tecmessa
For God's sake, don't betray us.

Ajax
I owe nothing to any god.

Tecmessa
Don't say that!

Ajax
Admonish those who can still hear you.

Tecmessa
Think of our son.

Ajax
I do
think of the child.

Tecmessa
I'm so afraid.

Ajax
Close up the tent after me.

Tecmessa
Ajax, please listen to your men.

Ajax
My men listen to me.

Tecmessa
Then listen to me.

Ajax
No one's going to change me now.

He goes, followed quickly by Tecmessa and the Boy.

Soldier
Beloved island
cyclonic rough
moderate or good
occasional rain.
Home
is the sound of waves
lapping the familiar shore –
gale warning
before the call to war.
Sometimes a street where I know every crack
the key turned in the door
to the sweet smells of baking
autumn leaves and lavender.

A girl I sat next to
is home
but not here:
Troy, Flanders, Basra, Helmand
those places where time wastes away
and men wear away
months and years beyond counting
staring at death.

Soldier

Here, Time whittles us down
to nothing.

CSM

And now I have to fear Ajax as well
led into his tent by some manic force.
Ajax the bravest of them all
but now brooding, alone, eating himself up
gone Elvis –
CR-PTSD'd,
boy do I hate this movie.
All his bravery in action
everything he's done
passed over by those Generals
who chose not to see what we've done.

Soldier

See his mother
white-haired, bent with age,
and now, woe, woe,
it's not sweet church hymns you'll hear
but the shrill shriek of her anguish
the thud of her hands beating her chest
the staccato snap of pulled-out hair.

Soldier

Ajax knows:
better to be dead

than sick like this, crazy.
He was the best of the lot.
Now he's not what he was
he's wandering beside himself.
We can't find him
in that empty look:
pulled back.
Ajax
who never pulls back
never knew the meaning
of withdrawal.

Soldier
And the dad,
what does he have to hear?
This was a respectable family,
no wreckage here before.
Only now.
His father hears the curse:
missing in action:
couldn't keep it together
waste of a son
the waste.

CSM
Tecmessa has followed him in
the medic
knows how to morphine pain.
Can she make him hear hope
when he's diddy-bopping in shame?

Soldier
If he won't give us orders
we have to obey them anyway.
What are his orders?

CSM
Get Teucer here
before it's too late.

Get Teucer here
even if it is too late.

The Soldiers go.

Odysseus and Athena come on.

Odysseus
What now?

Athena
Over to you, Odysseus.

Odysseus
Is he going to kill himself? That's what I would do.
I suppose it would give me a sense of control.

Athena
You're ten years into a war whose purpose you've
forgotten, you're a mass of contradictory voices
jangling in your shaking minds and you think you
have control? It's very touching.

Odysseus
Ajax is a commander.
He won't accept being a victim, even of his own mind.

Athena
We see you all as victims but then we take the long view.

Odysseus
It won't be good for the army if he kills himself. Can't
you stop him?

Athena
He doesn't hear me any more and anyway, pity is
a human trait, a very mysterious one too. Comes
and goes. Is that what you're feeling?

Odysseus
I can't feel pleased. He may be my enemy
but a mind once so cool now so wrecked –
and it's bad for army morale.

We know how to deal with the soldiers
when they crack – so they don't contaminate,
it's easy to get them out.
But Ajax?
Men will follow him anywhere –

Athena

The pan-piper of bravery
the heroic face of war:
completely useless.

Odysseus

That's what I think.

Athena

Of course you do.

Odysseus

But it's the dream of boys:
it's what brings them to us
and we don't train it out of them.
They all want to be like Ajax
even if they end up like me.
I have to go in and stop him. I can usually talk anyone
around to anything.

Athena

He could kill you.

Odysseus

That wouldn't be good for the army either.

Athena

And do you really want to stop him? Isn't he your
rival – an embittered one too?

Odysseus

I didn't stop his promotion. The Generals don't like
him anyway.
I only pointed out
he didn't always obey their orders.

Athena

One of these days, the Generals will notice he's their
bravest soldier.
You won't look good then
nor will your men get their medals.

Odysseus

Every muscle of my body, of my mind, trained to
compete.
It's the same muscles that make you win a war.
Soldiers have to want to win to survive.
Why is there always such a heavy price in the end?
Why does it feel so empty?

Athena

I'm not the goddess of introspection, I can't help you
there.
You're in a war, don't ask too many questions.

Odysseus

Facts, deduction.
The man's cracked up. The commander leads by
example.
If Ajax continues like this we'll soon have every soldier
in the army wandering around being sensitive and
complex.
Every infringement of discipline will be put down to
trauma,
every drunken brawl to combat stress, we won't have
an organism any more but a bunch of TUs claiming
it's not their temperament that's unsuitable for
battle but it's the battle that's unsuitable for their
temperaments.
Every decision will no longer be about how many men
we can afford to lose but how many minds we can
afford to stress. Might as well stop fighting now.
This won't do. I have to stop him. So. How?

Athena

You're usually better at thinking laterally.

Odysseus

I see: let him kill himself there in his tent, say it was
an accident, he was cleaning his rifle, no one will
believe it, keep repeating it so it seeps in, send his
men to a remote Forward Operating Base, no mobile
reception, no broadband, let them stay there for
months, get the body back home quietly, make sure
there are no cameras around. Got it, thank you, God.

Athena

War is never that simple. Here comes the friendly fire.
The deadly one.

Odysseus

General Menelaos. I have to stall him.

Menelaos comes on.

Menelaos

They've had one of their pow-wows.

They want compensation for each one of the goats
killed.

What they're asking for their goddamn goats would
break the military budget if we gave it to them.

And they want the man responsible.

I'll throw them that bone and keep them quiet until
we get them out of here and back to their villages
where we can bomb them in peace.

Not a very smart idea this practice village of yours,
Brigadier, they think it was a trick. So now they're
saying they'd like to act out a few suicide bombings
for our entertainment. Very funny. You've got us
into a fucking mess, get us out if it. I want the man
responsible in handcuffs. Who is it?

Odysseus

We're not sure, General, I've been asking the soldiers.

Menelaos

Find out fast and arrest him.

Odysseus

I don't have the authority to do that, sir.

Menelaos

I'm giving it to you.

Odysseus

It has to come from my own commanders.

Menelaos

Well, fucking get it.

Odysseus

It will take a little time.

Menelaos

We don't do time here. We have a war to win. Win it fast and get the hell out of here before we lose it again. This isn't helping.

Odysseus

I'll do my best, sir.

Menelaos

I want the man alive so I can hand him over to the ANA. No accidents. What happens then is none of my business.

Odysseus

Would it not be better for the army if we take care of this man ourselves, sir?

Menelaos

What the army needs is to win the war.

Odysseus

I agree, sir.

Menelaos

Well, what are you waiting for?

Odysseus

No one can win a war on their own, sir.

Athena

You might, you know, if you get a good idea.

Menelaos

Brigadier, *we* win this war. *You* get hold of the man
who killed the goats that's an order so we can hand
him over to the men with the goatees that's a pun
and be quick about it that's a command.

Odysseus leaves with Athena.

Menelaos

God, I'm so powerful and so smart.

He leaves. The Soldiers come on.

Ajax comes out with Tecmessa and his son.

Ajax

Time
stretching out oh so immense immeasurable
brings forth all things into the light,
and once revealed,
wraps them up again
in its night coat.
No surprises here:
the terrifying oath
the fierce will
can all be whittled down, made weak
soon to dissolve
in the rear-view mirror.
Look at me:
I was determined to do something terrible.
I held on to this with an iron will.
Now I'm softened, bent round,
spent like a woman
by a woman's tongue.

Moved to pity – can't bear to leave her
and my son an orphan.
But now let me go out of the gate
alone
and wash off these stains
in the desert dust.
I'll bury this weapon so deep no one can find it
and let darkness pull it down further even down to hell.
And then I'll know how to yield to any god
and to the higher authority of the Generals.
Why not?
Amazing how many things do yield to authority,
however powerful to begin with.
A bitter winter yields to a summer of soft fruits.
Fierce winds lull rough seas to sleep
and even sleep loosens its prey when consciousness
    knocks.
So then why shouldn't a man learn to be measured
    and tame?
And so I will. Roger.

Tecmessa

Ajax –
don't go out of the gate alone.
Take your men with you.

Ajax

A man's got to get away
got to be alone
gotta find a safe place
where there's no noise
and no one can approach him.

Tecmessa

There's always danger outside the base.

Ajax

No ambush
waits for the solitary man

but himself.
I'll take off my uniform
in the desert heat.
No one will know
this is Ajax.

Tecmessa

Let me come with you.

Ajax

Do what I fucking ask!
No one questions the Colonel's orders!
I solve the problems around here.
Split-second decisions, all mine
and if there's a fucking casualty, it's fucking mine.

To the Soldiers.

And you: wait here till Teucer comes
then ask him
to look after me well.
I repeat: to look after me well.
And after you too.

He goes to each of the men.

How's your foot? Completely healed? Get Tecmessa
to check it over.

To another.

I sorted the bank for you. Be more careful next time.

To another.

Don't argue with your girlfriend on the phone. You
have twenty minutes: reassure her: no descriptions,
except of sunsets.

To all.

You didn't chose this war
but now you're here, do it well.

Remember we can't predict a battle
but we have to know we can come back
and look at ourselves in the mirror
with pride.
That's what makes you my men.

He stops.

I'm going where I need to go.
I may be in pain now
but I'll find a way to save myself
and my honour.

Ajax goes. Tecmessa and the Boy as well.

Soldier
  Efrix! Hey –
  Bristling with hope
  swelling with joy
  I'm shuddering
  soaring.
  Hey there Pan
  great god Pan
  king of the dance
  trip down here
  from those ridges of snowy Arcadia
  and get me dancing
  cos
  I don't know these dances
  Yo Pan Pan
  get me dancing
  cos now it's my business
  to sing and dance.
  Look here comes another music god
  Apollo
  wafting over the seas
  left Delos
  crossing now –

drift over this way, God
give me the right steps
keep me dancing
safe through time.

Ares has softened
dissolved grief
from my eyes
oh oh now yes.
Now, O God
let the white light descend
the white light of the happy day
when we can get out of here
cos Ajax has come back
to himself to us
forgot his old pains.
Time blows up everything
even the anger of an Ajax.
Hope yeah hope
we got some hope around here –
Ajax is gonna forget his great quarrel –
and we're gonna get
some fragments of peace.

Athena comes on.

Soldier
Text message.

Soldier
The old man?

Soldier   Unknown. Base camp. OK. 'Teucer comes back
from the PSYOPS. Soon as he's in the camp, soldiers
circle him, insult his brother, Ajax, the crazy guy, the TU
traitor who's destroyed their safety. And that they'll both
be court-martialled by the JDCC and the CIMIC will send
them to the DTDF and no UNSCR for them. Teucer's about
to lose it but an RSM calms the situation. Where's Ajax?'

Soldier
Gone. Got a plan.

Soldier texts this.

Soldier
'Ajax has to stay in his tent.'

Soldier (*texts*)
Too late. Why?

Soldier
'Padre thinks God is angry.'

Soldier
Since when does the Padre think?

Soldier   'Cos he never prays and his men laugh at the blessing before patrols.'

Soldier
Tell the Padre to come here and join us on patrol.

Soldier texts this.

Soldier   From the Padre himself: 'Bodies that are great but without thought fall brutally at the hands of God when a man born with the limitations of human nature refuses to accept those limitations with his human mind.'

Soldier
What?

Athena
Let me translate this into simple concepts. You're born
   a man: think like a man.
Still don't understand? Ajax's father was a man who
   thought like a man. The day his son goes to war, he
   says to him:
'Son: fight bravely but always pray for the god's help.'
Not very complicated even for Ajax, you just say:
'Please God, help me kill the enemy.' Basic.

And do you know what that moron of a son answered?
'Father, a nobody can win if he has God's help. Well,
    I only trust myself and I'm gonna do it on my own.'
OK: he's young, he has a father complex, I let it pass
    because he's brave and I like that. But then:
We're in the middle of a tense battle right at the front,
    snipers everywhere. Compound's a hundred metres
    up over open ground. So I call to Ajax, hey there,
    Ajax, I'm here. I'll help you hold the line –
You know what he answers, that man, to me, God.
'You go and help those men over there. No line is
    gonna break anywhere I stand. I'm gonna make it
    to that compound on my own and clear the enemy.'

Well, that was it.
I'll say it again:
if you're born human, you better think like a human
otherwise you're on the path to destruction.
Ajax didn't do that,
he was stupid from the beginning,
forgot the limits of being human. Reality.
Now maybe you're thinking: how real are you?
Let's say: as long as I have power over you
I'm real – I hold in my wide arms
all that you can't contain in yourselves.
Back to Ajax:
I like bravery as much as any god.
But war is a collective effort,
got to think of others
not just your good name
that light of admiration in your men's eyes.
If you die you get the praises
the coveted name of hero
and you've left the men to fend for themselves.
Now I know war makes men lose all sense of themselves
and there's so much noise they go deaf anyway
but he went over.

Crack on is good,
go too far and I'll crack you.
God's logic.
Now look at Odysseus: he always has my voice in
   his head
See what I mean? He's coming. Heard me on the
   divine walkie- talkie.

Odysseus comes on.

Odysseus
   Where's Ajax?

Soldier
   Gone, sir.

Odysseus
   In his tent?

Soldier
   No, sir. Gone.

Odysseus
   What have you done with him?

Soldier
   Nothing, sir.

Odysseus
   You mean he's actually gone?

Soldier
   What I said, sir.

Odysseus
   Where did he go?

Soldier
   Tecmessa might know. Tecmessa!

Odysseus
   We can't have a madman wandering around on his
   own. Why didn't you stop him?

Soldier

He gave orders, sir.

Odysseus

And a whole fucking pack of scribes has just arrived,
looking for some story, one of their tragic myths,
makes them feel they've tasted combat but pity is
exactly what we don't want here anywhere or ever.

Athena

I like a good tragedy myself.

Odysseus

What am I going to do now?

Athena

All you can do is warn the Generals
but do it calmly, the army's stressed enough already.

Odysseus (*to the Soldiers*)

Has he gone out the gate?

Soldier

Didn't follow him, sir.

Odysseus

Stay where you are. Orders.

Soldier

From whom, sir?

Odysseus

From fucking above.

The men look up at the sky. Odysseus leaves quickly.

Athena

He won't forget that.

The men laugh. Tecmessa comes on.

Tecmessa

I was asleep, all worries receding like an ebbing tide
    on a soft day. Why did you call?

Soldier

We're getting messages.
This one's for you. Urgent.

Tecmessa

Ajax?

The Soldier hands over the phone.

Tecmessa

'Keep Ajax in his tent until sunset.'

Soldier

Same as what we're getting. Who the fuck's this guy?
    Ask him.

Tecmessa texts.

Tecmessa

He says he's the messenger:
'The next hours will decide between life and death.'

Soldier

Could be a joke.

Tecmessa

No. The golden hour when you can save someone . . .

Friends, protect me from the unfolding of events. The
next scene, I don't want to be in it. Find Ajax. Stop his
fateful footsteps. Get Teucer here. I was taken in by his
words, lulled into security. Wrong diagnosis. Child, we
can't wait here. No one will hurt you out there and you
can call him back. Let's go, be quick. Call the CSM.

Soldier

We know how to be quick: jacket, helmet, rifle, watch
    my speed.

Athena

These mortals rush about so and they still get the
timing wrong.

Outside the camp. Ajax on his own.

Ajax

Always stand in the strongest position.

He finds a spot, rifle ready, listening.

The last patrol.

He looks around.

All quiet, too quiet.
It's an ambush
fuck fuck fuck – from all sides.
The shell explodes
shrapnel cordite –
I hear the scream –
we have to move forward
under fire to the compound – comes the choice –
throw in a grenade
or force open the door
split-second decision:
put civilians at risk?
put my men at risk?
Option two this time, instinct.
In the room
a family
and the child with the wide-open eyes.
I never had a problem with the body parts
one leg here one leg there
like a film, seen it all
but the eyes of the child
age of my child
unfathomable openness
into the depth of terror

and the silent question
what is all this for?
Fear mirroring mine as I reflect his
in this hall of recurring fears.
I break down and cry:
maybe relief I didn't kill him
or do I already know I've lost three men?
And there's no medal for saving civilians
and for how long anyway? And who are they hiding?
If I'm his nightmare now how's he going to stop it?
Except one day do the same thing to me?
His eyes in flashback, always: better not to sleep.
The thing is: did I really see them?
Is it a film I can't remember? A picture?
In my brain, it all looks the same.
And sometimes I see the first option:
the grenade, as real as if it happened,
the dead child, ball in his hand
the film running parallel
and none of it is real
until you get killed. That's got to be real.

But it was never about the enemy
it was about me:
earn the respect of my men, earn the respect for my men.
Do the job well
come home look in the mirror feel OK
and never be ashamed
laughed at or pitied.
The hands that shake the shit that drips the fear that
    blinks the yell
pitched just too high
OK for others
but not for Ajax.
But where's the nobility
in the eyes of the child
who asks, what is all this all for?

Could I have saved the men?
Better not to sleep.

There were the good battles,
when I did everything right
no mistakes, perfect timing
judgement
brought the men safe back
but the fucking Generals saw nothing.

I call on the spirits of revenge
to visit the same destruction on them.
Give them years and years of rotting here
for nothing.
Only let my men go home.

He looks around.

It's too quiet, who's watching?
I'm asking you God to help me now.
I'm not asking to be recognised or appreciated or have
    medals or honours
or even be promoted, that's over.
All I'm asking is that you bring Teucer here
as soon as I've done what I have to.
I don't want the enemy to get here first
and mutilate me the way we mutilate theirs
in our grief and anger in this gangfuck of a war.
All I'm asking God
is a body brought home
with honour.

The day is bright it's gonna be hot –
I'm feeling the warmth for the last time
it must be real cold down there . . .

Hot afternoons at home
skimming stones rippling the water's surface.
The picture's all faded
bleached by the Asian sun

so called enemy land:
I never hated you
did what I had to do
for honour.
It's all about honour
isn't it?

Ajax puts his rifle to his mouth.

The Soldiers come on, very tentative. Covering their backs and each other.

Soldier

Ponos pono ponon ferei
pa pa.

Soldier

So this is my dream:
I'm swimming underwater and I find a door

Soldier

Over there, something moved –
can't see anything in this fucking dust –

Soldier

I swim into the room:
a body
completely covered with bandages from head to toe
surges towards me.
I panic and try to swim away.
He takes off his bandages
It's Ajax.

Soldier

Where is Ajax?
We're bum-fucking nowhere here
target for any sniper
might as well wave a flag.
Ajax!

CSM

Only man I know
not afraid of mines –

Soldier

only it got him in the end
the IED planted in his head.

CSM

Ajax!

Soldier

If we make too much noise
the Terries'll hear us
AK us 47
Ajax!

CSM

Over there!

They fall to the ground. Freeze.

Soldier

I was happy to die for him
but without him:
No.

Soldier

He'll lead us back
always has.

Soldier

When he was Ajax.
Not so sure now.

CSM

He's always known what's right.
Always cracked on
never cracked.
Ajax!

Tecmessa
Io moi moi!

CSM
A high-pitched cry over there –

Soldier
There was a cry in my dream –

CSM
Get down!

Soldier
It's a woman.

CSM
I don't care if it's a fucking mermaid. Get down!

Tecmessa
Io, whoa.

CSM
It's Tecmessa.

Tecmessa
Here!
Ajax.

Soldier
Asleep?

Tecmessa
The black blood spurts like an evil fountain.

Soldier
What do we do now?

Tecmessa
Where is Teucer?

Soldier
He spilled his blood alone
no mates to look after him.

CSM

He was never going to bend.
Not Ajax. Should've known.
Invincible Ajax.

Tecmessa

Wait till they need him again.
These people don't know they have a good thing until
    it's gone.
Sweet to them his death maybe but bitter to me –
but sweet to Ajax too,
what he wanted
longed for.
No one will laugh at him now.
Whatever he saw, he saw it clearly
and did what he had to.
Teucer will come
look after you, your son.
And for me? Now. Nothing.
I lose everything, once again.
Gone the comfort of a deep loved voice,
no sound in my head but the wind.

CSM

There's a broken sound, off –
tunes itself to the wreckage here.

Soldier

Teucer.

Teucer comes on. Looks for a moment.

Teucer

Is this my brother's body?

CSM

You can see: Ajax is dead.

Teucer

So the rumours in the army prove themselves true.

CSM

So it is.

Teucer

Hasty deed.

CSM

When did Ajax ever hesitate?

Teucer

What about the child, where is he?

Tecmessa gestures.

Bring him here. One of our enemies could snatch him –
like a cub from the wounded lioness –
leaving her bereft. Quick –
I will defend this body from any carrion crow that
   wants it as food or fodder.

Tecmessa leaves.

Uncover him so I can see the damage.
You die, brother, but do you know how many sorrows
   come to life
for the rest of us?
For me?
What am I going to say to our father, Telamon?
What kind of a happy expression am I going to see
   on his face when I appear without Ajax. Telamon
   never cracks a smile even when he's doing well.
He won't keep his words back
not to his illegitimate son
born to a girl in one of the lands he occupied,
taken in from pity or guilt.
He'll call me a coward for not looking after you
say that I betrayed you because I'm not a man
or maybe even worse that I'm the one who by deceit
tried to get your inheritance.

Telamon always quick to anger now loses his temper
    over the smallest thing
more and more oppressive as he gets older.
And finally, he'll push me away, throw me out and
    his words will shrivel me to nothing.
That's at home.
What about here?
I have many enemies here.
My strength vanishes with your death.
What can I do now?
What voices, brother,
were you hearing when you did this?
What god?
Why wasn't I here?
And now,
how am I going to honour your body?

CSM

Be quick – someone's bound to come.

Teucer

The body has to be brought back to the camp
publicly,
with military honour.

Tecmessa and the Boy enter.

Child, stand guard over your father's body. Hold his
    weapon. There.
And you, don't be cowards and run away. Stay by
    this body until I we find a suitable way to bring
    Ajax back. Tecmessa, come with me.

Teucer goes with Tecmessa.

Soldier

How much longer?
How many more years?
windswept

on the Asian plains
the dust of Helmand
the sand of Troy
salt marshes of Basra
the barren rocks of Aden
Bosnia
The jungle of Malaya
Vietnam
The beaches of Al Faw.

How much longer?
the ceaseless misery
unending war work.

I wish he'd never existed
or went down to hell before he lived
that man
who first taught us warfare.
Hardship leading to more hardship
that man ruined all men
oh ponoi progonoi ponon
and pain promotes more pain.

No pleasure for me here
no party hats drink music
not even the sweetness of a good night's sleep
and as for love. Love. Oimoi
he sure stopped all that:
I lie neglected
alone
in my cold fartsack
my hair streaked with desert frost
and wake up to this shithole.

Home, I want to go home,
feel the lapping of the sea
flowering fruit trees
the smell of autumn leaves

Magnum cider *with ice*
the green criss-cross patches of England
when you fly in.

Teucer comes in with Tecmessa.

Teucer

We have what we need.
We'll lay him on this.
After we've washed the body.

Soldier

Hurry because here comes one of the four-stars, the
worst. General Menelaos – whose shattered
manhood and confused country we're fighting to
shore up.

Menelaos comes on.

Menelaos

Keep your hands off that corpse. You're not moving
him anywhere.

Teucer

What could such a long and gracious speech mean?

Menelaos

It ain't a speech, it's an order.

Teucer

We need orders to make sense.

Menelaos

He joined our army as a friend and ally. But he's a
worse enemy than the real enemy we're fighting.
He plotted our death. He crept up on us at night
to get rid of us and if God hadn't stopped him
I would've ended up like he is now.
Brains scattered all over the place
and he'd be living and exulting.

But as it is he couldn't tell the difference between a
    biped and a quadruped – that's the joke going
    around –
not surprising where he comes from –
it's all that officer training you have
in those black hills those little mountains of yours
spying on herds I hear.
And you treat your animals like humans.
And vice versa.
He must've remembered his training.
So now he's going to remain here and feed the vultures
    and the hyenas.
Because he's no hero but a suicide
and we don't like that.
Not good for army morale.
Don't try any heroics on me.
He didn't listen to anybody when he was alive.
Now that he's dead he'll do what I say.
It's not good when officers
decide they're not going to follow the orders of the
    higher command.
This man was hot-headed, insolent, much too big for
    his boots.
I'm the only one around here who has a right to talk big.
And I tell you you're not going anywhere with that
    body and the only coffin that's gonna be flown out
    of here is yours.

Teucer

Ajax came as your ally but under our command.
By what right do you give orders here?
It was never agreed that we could order you about
or that you could order us about.
So command what you can command.
Tell you own soldiers how to behave.
Ajax didn't come here for your sake or to defend the
    pride of your country.

73

He came because he'd sworn an oath to be your ally
    and he was bound by that oath.
He never had much respect for nobodies.
And my duty is to honour Ajax's remains
whether you like it or not.

Menelaos

Is it right for Ajax to be treated with honour after
    killing me?

Teucer

I didn't notice I was speaking to a ghost.

Menelaos

But for the grace of God I would be.

Teucer

Well, don't dishonour the god who saved you.

Menelaos

He dishonoured himself: suicide is the act of a coward.

Teucer

Then perhaps you shouldn't send us on so many
    suicide missions.

Menelaos

He hated me. Everybody knows it.

Teucer

Maybe when he discovered you were blocking his way

Menelaos

I didn't promote Odysseus, there's a board.

Teucer

There's many ways of abusing influence.

Menelaos

This is the last time I'm saying it, this corpse will not
    be honoured.

Teucer

And I'm telling you, this man's body will be treated
with the respect it deserves.

Menelaos

No point talking: I'm going to get some reinforcement.

Teucer

Some of that friendly fire of yours?

Menelaos

Listen: half-breed.
Yes, you.
Maybe if you were one of us you could use these high
and mighty tones and strut about
but you're nothing.
Hear?

Teucer

We can always hear you.

Menelaos

Good.

Teucer

But sometimes we find it hard to understand
what you're trying to communicate.

Menelaos

I'm saying: he was nothing.
These big reckless men aren't the most clever:
when you have a broad-backed ox you need to use
a whip
and I think that's what you need too to get some sense
into your nous.
Ajax is a ghost now
invisible, air, not there.
Try to hide behind his big back?
But you're the one we see.
How dare you speak like a commander?
Learn who you are before you speak to us.

Anyway when you speak I don't understand a word
cos I don't understand the words of half-breeds.
And Ajax is gonna stay right here, R&F: rotten and
forgotten.

Teucer

Ajax: this general can't remember how many times
you risked your life for his sake.
He's tossed all that away.
So, General, what can't you remember?
The time the battle turned against you and you
retreated to the safety of the compound?
And there was the enemy coming after you –
shells and mortars raining down –
who kept fighting?
Wasn't it Ajax?
Who was always the one who volunteered for patrol?
Wasn't it a relief it was Ajax
and that it was Ajax and his brave men
who would leave the base and deal with an IED
without waiting hours for the disposal team?
Who thought strategy in the furthest FOBs
when you were back here worrying about the length
of sideburns
worrying we were losing the war because of sideburns
said you didn't want Elvis cutting around Afghanistan
as if that was more important than whether we could
shoot straight.
And Ajax always had compassion for any of his men
whose stash of courage had run low
but where's yours when you see this man
whom nothing could break but injustice?
If you try to keep us from honouring his body
you'll have to kill us all.
I'd rather die openly for Ajax than
for the sake of your country's bent honour
or your fear of an alien god.

Odysseus comes on with Athena.

Athena
They have a war to win and they're fighting each other.
Happens all the time.
Odysseus, I still don't understand human behaviour
and I'm eternal.
You better do something.

Odysseus
The whole army can hear the shouting over this corpse.

Menelaos
I've been reprimanding this man for his disrespect.

Odysseus
How is he being disrespectful?

Menelaos
He wants this body sent home with full honours
instead of leaving it to rot as it should.

Odysseus
Could I say a few words without being disrespectful?

Menelaos
Sure. We got you promoted: you're a friend.

Odysseus
Listen then. Don't let this soldier remain unburied in
such a pitiless manner,
letting his body rot in public – holes pecked by
scavenging birds,
gnawed flesh shrinking in shame
or worse, used by the enemy as fodder for their
mockery –
dismembered, abused, we've seen rage push men's
invention into scenes beyond horror – unimaginable
acts on undefended bodies – shreds of humanity
dripping from poles –

Don't let that happen to Ajax.

Honour the soldier who fought for you.

And don't be so overpowered by your hatred of him
   that you trample justice underfoot.

Ajax was my enemy but I wouldn't want to take my
   revenge

by lying about him now and denying his greatness.

It's not right to dishonour a man of such worth, even
   if you hate him.

Menelaos

So now Odysseus, you've changed sides? You're his
   buddy suddenly?

Odysseus

I hated him when it was right to hate him.

Menelaos

Then why not kick him when he's down?

Odysseus

Don't try to enjoy, General, satisfactions which are
   not right.

Menelaos

It's for the superior officer to make decisions.

Odysseus

You become superior by deciding what's right.

Menelaos

This man was a pain in the ass from the start. You
   told us so yourself.

Odysseus

That's usually the case with great heroes.

Menelaos

But how can you respect a guy who hated you?

Odysseus

His excellence weighs more heavily than his antagonism.

Menelaos
Changing your mind shows weakness.

Odysseus
Stubbornness isn't praiseworthy either.

Menelaos
You're going to make me look weak.

Odysseus
No, only honourable.

Menelaos
Listen, Odysseus
People like us can't change our minds.
Or ever admit we were wrong
otherwise we'd have to resign.

Odysseus
You can bring in new evidence:
shift the words a bit.
Tragic accident, human frailty, reversal of fortune,
bad luck – blame that on God,
then move on to legend.
This man is already a legend and we need legends
    in this war.

Menelaos
So you're telling me to have the body sent home.

Odysseus
Yes, because I'll be in the same position one day and
    I would want to be honoured.

Menelaos
Well then let it be your decision not mine.

Odysseus
You're being magnanimous to allow it.

Menelaos
I'll do a lot for you but I still hate that man.

Athena

This is war: his life is gone. Honour the body. Hear?

Menelaos

I got it the first time!

Odysseus

I didn't say anything.

Menelaos

Fucking hell, I'm hearing voices.

Menelaos leaves. Odysseus stays.

Odysseus

Teucer, as much as I was once an enemy, I'm ready
to be a friend.

And I wish to join you in honouring Ajax. I'll spare
no pains for the sake of the best and bravest of men.

Teucer

Odysseus,

you're renowned yourself for your bravery and I can
only praise you for your words.

You put a lie to my expectations.

You were his worst enemy but you stood by him and
you didn't try to insult or humiliate him once he
was dead.

Unlike that thunderous empty-headed General

who wanted to abuse his body and throw it to the dogs.

May God and those millepede war furies who forget
nothing bring the whole lot down in the same way
they tried to bring Ajax down.

But now, Odysseus, I'm afraid to let you touch this
body – or get too close –

in case Ajax should find this intolerable –

But help us in any other way and ask our soldiers to
come and assist us.

And know that I salute you as a man of real worth.

Odysseus
I would have liked to help more.
I would have been honoured to walk behind the body
when you take him back to the camp.
But I will respect what you ask
on behalf of Ajax.

He leaves.

Teucer
Child, come over here
and use whatever strength you have to help me lift
    him up.
But first place a loving hand on your father.
There was no greater hero anywhere
than this big, this brave soldier, Ajax.

Soldier
Soldiers experience and understand many things
but we can never guess in advance how we'll act.

Acknowledgements

I would like to thank

Colonel David Roe
Major Richard Streatfeild
Lieutenant-Colonel Richard (Skid) Dorney
Professor Simon Wessely
Professor Christopher Dandeker
Danny McEneany
Veterans in Prison
Combat Stress
Aly Renwick
Purni Morell
Margaret Williamson
The Peggy Ramsay Foundation
The Freud Museum
Peggy Shannon and the Women and War project
Karl Sydow